BEAT THE ODDS:

CASINO STRATEGIES

FOR GUARANTEED

WINS

FOR SERIOUS

PLAYERS

Grant Howard

Table of Contents

Introduction 1

Chapter 1: Know Thy Enemy: The Casino's Edge 2

Chapter 2: Money Matters: Bankroll Management for Survival 5

Chapter 3: Choosing Your Battles: Games with the Best Odds 7

Chapter 4: Betting Smart: Strategies for Every Bankroll 10

Chapter 5: Beyond the Felt: Tips, Tricks, and Mindset 15

Chapter 6: Real-World Examples: Success Stories and Lessons Learned 20

Conclusion 26

Appendices 27

Glossary of Casino Terms

Recommended Reading and Resources

Self-Assessment: Are You a Responsible Gambler 29

Introduction

Why This Book Matters: The Illusion of Easy Money

Casinos are designed to be dazzling, filled with flashing lights, ringing bells, and the compelling promise of quick riches. But behind the glitz and glamour lies a carefully calculated system designed to extract money from players. This book aims to pull back the curtain and reveal the truth about casino gambling, empowering you with the knowledge to make informed decisions and increase your chances of winning.

A Different Approach: Strategies, Not Systems

Forget the get-rich-quick schemes and "foolproof" systems promising instant wealth. This book focuses on practical strategies that can be applied to various casino games, giving you a real edge over the house. We'll delve into the mathematics of gambling, the psychology of decision-making, and the importance of discipline and self-control.

Responsible Gambling: The Foundation of Winning

Winning at the casino isn't just about luck but responsible gambling. This means setting limits, sticking to a budget, and never chasing losses. We'll explore the dangers of problem gambling and provide resources for those who need help. Remember, gambling should be a fun activity, not a destructive force in your life.

Chapter 1: Know Thy Enemy: The Casino's Edge

The House Always Wins (But By How Much?): Understanding House Edge

Every casino game has a built-in advantage for the house, known as the house edge. This is the percentage of each bet the casino expects to keep over the long run. Understanding the house edge is crucial for choosing the right games and making informed betting decisions. Let's break it down:

- **Blackjack:** With a basic strategy, the house edge can be as low as 0.5%.
- **Baccarat:** The house edge on the banker bet is around 1.06%.
- **Roulette (American):** The house edge is 5.26% due to the double zero (00).
- **Roulette (European):** The house edge is 2.70% with a single zero.
- **Slot Machines:** The house edge varies widely but can range from 2% to 15%.
- **Keno:** Keno has a high house edge, often around 25%.

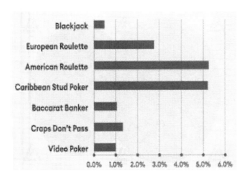

Knowing the house edge allows you to choose games where you have a better chance of winning and avoid those where the odds are heavily stacked against you.

It's Not Just Luck: How Casinos Stack the Odds

Casinos employ various tactics to maximize their profits and keep players engaged:

- **Casino Layout:** Casinos are designed like mazes, with winding paths and strategically placed distractions to keep you inside and gambling.
- **Lighting and Sound:** The bright lights and stimulating sounds create an exciting atmosphere that can make you lose track of time and money.
- **Free Drinks:** Complimentary drinks are offered to lower your inhibitions and encourage risk-taking.
- **No Clocks or Windows:** Casinos intentionally avoid clocks and windows to disorient you and make you lose track of time.
- **Near Misses:** Slot machines are programmed to produce near misses, which give you the illusion of almost winning and entice you to keep playing.

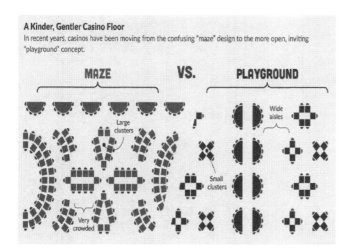

A Kinder, Gentler Casino Floor
In recent years, casinos have been moving from the confusing "maze" design to the more open, inviting "playground" concept.

By being aware of these tactics, you can resist their influence and make more rational decisions while gambling.

3

Your Best Weapon: Knowledge is Power

The more you know about casino games, the better equipped you'll be to make intelligent choices and avoid costly mistakes. Research the rules, odds, and strategies for the games you plan to play. Practice online or with friends to gain experience before risking real money. Remember, knowledge is power in the casino, and the more you learn, the better your chances of winning.

Chapter 2: Money Matters: Bankroll Management for Survival

The Golden Rule: Only Gamble What You Can Afford to Lose

Imagine walking into a casino with a month's rent, grocery money, or even your child's college savings. The pressure is immense. Every loss feels like a catastrophe; every bet is tinged with desperation. This is the antithesis of intelligent gambling. The golden rule is simple: only bring money you're prepared to kiss goodbye. Treat it like entertainment spending, the cost of a fun night out. If you win, fantastic! If not, it won't ruin your life. This mindset shift is essential for making rational decisions at the table.

Budgeting for Success: More Than Just Cash in Hand

Bankroll management isn't just about how much money you have; it's about how you manage it. Set a daily, weekly, or monthly gambling budget and stick to it religiously. Divide your bankroll into smaller sessions, each with its limit. This prevents you from chasing losses and blowing your entire budget in one go. Think of it as pacing yourself during a marathon – you don't sprint at the start, and you conserve energy for the long haul.

Winning and Losing Streaks: How to Ride Them Out

Every gambler experiences winning and losing streaks. It's the nature of the game. But how you react to these streaks can make all the difference. When you're winning, don't get overconfident and increase your bets recklessly. Set a win goal and walk away when you reach it. When you're losing, don't chase your losses by doubling down or making impulsive bets. Accept that luck isn't always on your side and take a break. Remember, the goal is to enjoy yourself and minimize losses, not to win every hand.

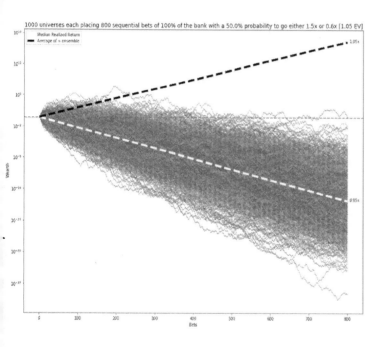

The Walk-Away Point: Knowing When to Quit

This is perhaps the most crucial aspect of bankroll management. Knowing when to quit is as important as knowing when to bet. Set a loss limit before you start gambling, and stick to it, no matter what. It's easy to get caught up in the excitement of the game and lose track of time and money. But if you hit your loss limit, walk away. Don't try to win it back in one desperate bet. Remember, there will always be another day, and the casino will always be there waiting.

Chapter 3: Choosing Your Battles: Games with the Best Odds

Blackjack: Skill Beats Luck (If You Play Smart)

Blackjack, often referred to as "21," is a card game that offers some of the best odds in the casino. Unlike pure luck-based games like slots, blackjack involves strategic decision-making that can significantly impact your chances of winning. By learning basic strategy, which consists of knowing the optimal move for every possible hand combination, you can reduce the house edge to less than 1%. This means that for every $100 you wager, you're only expected to lose less than $1 over the long run.

However, mastering blackjack takes time and practice. You must memorize the basic strategy chart and apply it consistently to every hand. But the rewards are worth the effort – skilled blackjack players can consistently win money over time.

YOUR HAND	DEALER'S CARD									
	2	3	4	5	6	7	8	9	10	A
8	H	H	H	H	H	H	H	H	H	H
9	H	D/H	D/H	D/H	D/H	H	H	H	H	H
10	D/H	D/H	D/H	D/H	D/H	D/H	D/H	D/H	H	H
11	D/H	D/H	D/H	D/H	D/H	D/H	D/H	D/H	D/H	D/H
12	H	H	S	S	S	H	H	H	H	H
13	S	S	S	S	S	H	H	H	H	H
14	S	S	S	S	S	H	H	H	H	H
15	S	S	S	S	S	H	H	H	R/H	H
16	S	S	S	S	S	H	H	R/H	R/H	R/H
17	S	S	S	S	S	S	S	S	S	S
A,2	H	H	H	D/H	D/H	H	H	H	H	H
A,3	H	H	H	D/H	D/H	H	H	H	H	H
A,4	H	H	D/H	D/H	D/H	H	H	H	H	H
A,5	H	H	D/H	D/H	D/H	H	H	H	H	H
A,6	H	D/H	D/H	D/H	D/H	H	H	H	H	H
A,7	S	D/S	D/S	D/S	D/S	S	S	H	H	H
A,8	S	S	S	S	S	S	S	S	S	S
2,2	P/H	P/H	P	P	P	P	H	H	H	H
3,3	P/H	P/H	P	P	P	P	H	H	H	H
4,4	H	H	H	P/H	P/H	H	H	H	H	H
5,5	D/H	D/H	D/H	D/H	D/H	D/H	D/H	D/H	H	H
6,6	P/H	P	P	P	P	H	H	H	H	H
7,7	P	P	P	P	P	P	H	H	H	H
8,8	P	P	P	P	P	P	P	P	P	P
9,9	P	P	P	P	P	S	P	P	S	S
10,10	S	S	S	S	S	S	S	S	S	S
A,A	P	P	P	P	P	P	P	P	P	P

Legend:

- **H** — hit
- **S** — stand
- **P** — split
- **D/H** — double down if possible, otherwise hit
- **D/S** — double down if possible, otherwise stand
- **P/H** — split if double down after split is possible, otherwise hit
- **R/H** — surrender if possible, otherwise hit

Baccarat: Simplicity with a Surprisingly Low Edge

Baccarat is a popular card game known for its simplicity and elegance. It involves betting whether the player or banker will have a hand closer to nine. The game offers three possible outcomes: a player win, a banker win, or a tie. While the house edge is slightly higher for the banker bet (due to a 5% commission), it remains one of the lowest in the casino. Baccarat requires no skill or strategy; the outcome is purely based on chance. This makes it an excellent option for beginners or those who prefer a less complex game.

Video Poker: Slots with a Twist of Strategy

Video poker combines elements of slot machines and poker, offering a unique blend of luck and strategy. While the game is ultimately based on random card draws, players can make decisions that affect the outcome, such as which cards to hold and which to discard. By learning the optimal strategy for each video poker variant, you can significantly reduce the house edge and even achieve a positive expected value in some cases. However, finding these favorable variants can be challenging, and it requires discipline to stick to the optimal strategy. Jacks or Better is a good game to start out with because the volatility is lower compared to other variations.

ROYAL FLUSH	250	500	750	1000	4000
STRAIGHT FLUSH	50	100	150	200	250
4 OF A KIND	25	50	75	100	125
FULL HOUSE	9	18	27	36	45
FLUSH	6	12	18	24	30
STRAIGHT	4	8	12	16	20
3 OF A KIND	3	6	9	12	15
TWO PAIR	2	4	6	8	10
JACK OR BETTER	1	2	3	4	5

The Traps to Avoid: Slot Machines, Keno, and More

While some casino games offer decent odds, others should be avoided altogether. Slot machines, for instance, have a notoriously high house edge, often exceeding 10%. This means that for every $100 you wager, you can expect to lose $10 or more over time. Keno, a lottery-style game, is even worse, with a house edge that can reach up to 30%. Roulette, while exciting, also favors the house, especially the American version with its double zero. These games rely heavily on luck, and no strategy can overcome the built-in disadvantage. Stick to games with lower house edges and better odds to maximize your chances of winning. However, if you're determined to play slots, some machines offer better odds than others. Look for games with higher payback percentages and avoid progressive jackpot slots, as the odds of winning the jackpot are extremely slim. Some players swear by specific machines like Top Dollar, Pinball, and Red, White, and Blue Sevens, claiming they offer better chances of winning than others. While no scientific evidence supports these claims, if you find a machine that seems to be paying out more often, stick with it and see if your luck continues. Remember, playing slots is ultimately a game of chance, and there's no guarantee of winning. But by choosing the right machines and managing your bankroll wisely, you can at least minimize your losses and extend your playtime.

Chapter 4: Betting Smart: Strategies for Every Bankroll

Martingale: Doubling Down on Risk

The Martingale system is a popular yet controversial betting strategy often used in games like roulette or craps. The premise is simple: double your bet after each loss, aiming to eventually win back your losses and make a profit. In theory, this sounds appealing. After all, if you keep doubling your bet, you're bound to win eventually, right? Unfortunately, the reality is far more complex.

The Martingale system has several significant flaws:

- **Limited Bankroll:** Doubling your bet repeatedly can quickly drain your bankroll, especially if you encounter a losing streak. Even a modest starting bet can escalate into astronomical amounts after a few losses.

- **Table Limits:** Most casinos have table limits, meaning there's a maximum amount you can bet on a single hand or spin. This can prevent you from doubling your bet indefinitely, effectively cutting short your Martingale strategy.

- **The Gambler's Fallacy:** The Martingale system is based on the false belief that past outcomes influence future results. Just because you've lost several hands in a row doesn't mean you're "due" for a win. Each hand or spin is independent, and the odds remain the same.

Despite these drawbacks, the Martingale system can be tempting, especially for those seeking quick wins. However, it's essential to understand the risks involved and use it cautiously, if at all.

Paroli: Riding the Winning Wave

Unlike the Martingale system, which focuses on recovering losses, the Paroli system aims to capitalize on winning streaks. With this strategy, you double your bet after each win, riding the wave of good fortune. If you lose, you reset your bet to the original amount. The Paroli system is considered less risky than the Martingale because it doesn't require a large bankroll to implement. However, it still relies on luck and the unpredictable nature of winning streaks.

Here's how the Paroli system works:

1. Start with a base bet.
2. If you win, double your bet on the next hand.
3. If you win again, double your bet again.
4. Continue doubling your bet after each win until you reach a predetermined number of consecutive wins (usually three or four).
5. Once you reach your target, reset your bet to the original amount and start the cycle again.

6. If you lose at any point, reset your bet to the original amount.

The Paroli system can be a fun and potentially profitable way to gamble, but it's important to remember that winning streaks can end abruptly. Don't get carried away and risk your winnings by chasing an elusive streak.

Table of Outcomes for Paroli Betting System

FIRST BET	SECOND BET	THIRD BET	NET RESULT
-1 Loss	-1 Loss	-1 Loss	- 3
-1 Loss	-1 Loss	+1 Win*	- 1
-1 Loss	+1 Win	-2 Loss	- 2
-1 Loss	+1 Win	+2 Win*	+ 2
+1 Win	-2 Loss	-1 Loss	- 2
+1 Win	-2 Loss	+1 Win*	+/- 0
+1 Win	+2 Win	-4 Loss	- 1
+1 Win	+2 Win	+4 Win	+ 7

* Progression to continue

Flat Betting: Consistency for the Cautious

Flat betting is the simplest and most conservative betting strategy. It involves betting the same amount on every hand or spin, regardless of previous outcomes. While this may seem boring, it's a safe and effective way to manage your bankroll, especially for beginners or those with limited funds.

Flat betting eliminates the risk of rapidly depleting your bankroll during losing streaks, allowing you to enjoy the game without the stress of constantly adjusting your bets. While flat betting won't lead to massive wins, it's a sustainable strategy that can help you stay in the game longer and potentially walk away with a profit. It's a good option for those who prioritize consistency and risk management over the thrill of chasing big wins.

When to Bet Big, When to Lay Low: Adjusting Your Strategy

In the ever-changing landscape of casino games, adapting your betting strategy is crucial for maximizing your potential winnings and minimizing losses. While flat betting provides a stable foundation, knowing when to increase or decrease your bets can significantly impact your overall success.

Increasing Your Bets:

There are strategic moments when increasing your bets can be advantageous:

- **Positive Progression Systems:** These systems involve increasing your bet after a win, with the idea of capitalizing on hot streaks. Examples include the Paroli system, where you double your bet after each win, and the 1-3-2-6 system, where you increase your bet in a specific sequence following wins.

ROUND	BET	IF WIN	IF LOSE
1	1 on Player	Net win 1	Net loss 1, start over
2	3 on Player	Total net win 4	Total net loss 2, start over
3	2 on Player	Total net win 6	Total net win 2, start over
4	6 on Player	Total net win 12	Break even, start over

- **High Confidence:** If you're playing a skill-based game like blackjack and have a strong hand or favorable count, increasing your bet can lead to larger payouts.
- **Favorable Table Conditions:** In some games, like baccarat, you may notice patterns or trends that suggest a particular outcome is more likely. In these cases, increasing your bet can be a calculated risk.

Decreasing Your Bets:

Conversely, there are situations where it's wise to decrease your bets:

- **Losing Streaks:** If you're on a losing streak, it's crucial to scale back your bets to protect your bankroll. Chasing losses by increasing your bets is a recipe for disaster.

- **Negative Progression Systems:** These systems involve decreasing your bet after a loss, with the aim of minimizing losses during cold streaks. The Martingale system is an example of a negative progression system, but it's important to use it cautiously due to its inherent risks.

- **Uncertainty:** If you're unsure of the optimal strategy or feel like you're losing your edge, it's wise to decrease your bets until you regain your confidence or find a more favorable game.

The Key to Success:

The key to adjusting your betting strategy is finding the right balance between aggression and caution. It's essential to be flexible and adapt to the changing dynamics of the game. Don't be afraid to experiment with different betting strategies and find what works best for you. Remember, the goal is to maximize your winnings while minimizing losses, and adjusting your bets can be a powerful tool in achieving that goal.

Chapter 5: Beyond the Felt: Tips, Tricks, and Mindset

Comp It Up: Freebies Aren't Always a Good Deal

Casinos are notorious for showering players with freebies – complimentary drinks, meals, hotel rooms, and even show tickets. These perks, known as "comps," are designed to entice you to gamble more and stay longer. While it's tempting to indulge in these freebies, it's important to remember that there's no such thing as a free lunch. Casinos factor in the cost of comps when calculating their profits, and they're not giving them away out of the goodness of their hearts.

Before you accept a comp, consider the following:

- **The Value of the Comp:** Is the freebie genuinely worth the amount of money you're expected to gamble to earn it? If you're a low-stakes player, a free buffet might not be worth it if you have to wager hundreds of dollars to qualify.
- **Your Gambling Habits:** Do you tend to gamble more when you've had a few drinks? If so, free beverages might not be in your best interest.
- **Alternative Options:** Could you get a better deal elsewhere? For example, instead of accepting a free hotel room at the casino, could you find a more affordable accommodation nearby?

While comps can enhance your casino experience, it's crucial to weigh the pros and cons and avoid getting caught up in the allure of freebies. Remember, the goal is to leave the casino with more money than you came with, not just a handful of free trinkets.

Players' Clubs: Loyalty Has Its Perks

Most casinos offer players' clubs or loyalty programs that reward you for your gambling activity. By signing up for a players' club and using your membership card while you play, you can earn points that can be redeemed for various rewards, such as cashback, free play, discounts on dining and accommodations, and even exclusive invitations to events.

While players' clubs can be a great way to get more value out of your gambling experience, it's crucial to understand how they work. The rewards you earn are typically based on how much you gamble and the types of games you play. Casinos track your activity through your membership card, so they know exactly how much you're wagering and which games you prefer.

Before you join a players' club, consider the following:

14

- **The Rewards Structure:** Are the rewards offered worth the effort? Some casinos have more generous programs than others.

- **Your Gambling Habits:** Do you gamble frequently enough to earn significant rewards? If you only visit the casino occasionally, a players' club might not be worth it.

- **Privacy Concerns:** Are you comfortable with the casino tracking your gambling activity? Some players prefer to remain anonymous.

f you decide to join a players' club, read the terms and conditions carefully. Pay attention to how points are earned and redeemed, and be aware of any expiration dates or other restrictions.

Stay Sharp: The Dangers of Alcohol and Fatigue

Casinos are designed to be immersive environments that transport you away from the everyday world. The constant stimulation, the clinking of chips, the whirring of slot machines, and the flowing alcohol can all contribute to a sense of euphoria and disorientation. While a few drinks might seem like a harmless way to loosen up and have fun, alcohol can significantly impair your judgment and decision-making abilities.

Under the influence of alcohol, you're more likely to:

- **Take unnecessary risks:** You might bet more than you intended or chase losses you wouldn't usually chase.
- **Make impulsive decisions:** You might deviate from your strategy or bet on hunches rather than logic
- **Lose track of time and money:** The hours can fly by when you're having fun, but the longer you gamble, the more likely you will lose.

Similarly, fatigue can also cloud your judgment and lead to poor decision-making. When you're tired, your ability to concentrate and think clearly diminishes, making you more susceptible to mistakes. It's important to be mindful of your energy levels and take breaks when needed. Don't try to push through exhaustion; it's not worth jeopardizing your bankroll.

Here are some tips for staying sharp at the casino:

- **Limit your alcohol intake:** If you choose to drink, do so in moderation. Set a limit for yourself and stick to it.
- **Stay hydrated:** Drink plenty of water to avoid dehydration, which can contribute to fatigue.
- **Take breaks:** Step away from the tables or machines every hour or so to clear your head and stretch your legs.
- **Get enough sleep:** Aim for 7-8 hours of sleep before heading to the casino.
- **Eat regular meals:** Don't gamble on an empty stomach. A well-nourished body and mind are essential for making sound decisions.

By taking care of yourself and staying sharp, you'll be better equipped to make rational choices, stick to your strategy, and ultimately increase your chances of winning at the casino.

The Psychology of Gambling: Avoiding Tilt and Chasing Losses

Gambling is not just a game of chance; it's also a game of emotions. The highs of winning and the lows of losing can trigger a rollercoaster of feelings, from elation and excitement to frustration and despair. Understanding the psychology of gambling is crucial for maintaining composure and making rational decisions, even under pressure.

One of the most common pitfalls for gamblers is "tilt." Tilt is a state of emotional or mental frustration in which a player adopts a less-than-optimal strategy, usually resulting in irrational decision-making and increased losses. Tilt can be triggered by a bad beat, a losing streak, or simply a frustrating situation at the table.

Another common trap is chasing losses. This is when a player tries to recoup losses by increasing their bets or deviating from their strategy. Chasing losses is a dangerous path that can quickly lead to financial ruin.

Here are some tips for avoiding tilt and chasing losses:

- **Recognize the signs:** Be aware of your emotional state and take a break if you start to feel frustrated, angry, or stressed.
- **Take a step back:** If you're on a losing streak, walk away from the table or machine and clear your head.
- **Set loss limits:** Determine how much you're willing to lose before you start gambling and stick to it.
- **Don't gamble to escape problems:** Gambling should be a fun and entertaining activity, not a way to cope with stress or emotional issues.

- **Seek help if needed:** If you're struggling with problem gambling, don't hesitate to seek professional help. There are many resources available to help you overcome addiction and regain control of your life.

By understanding the psychology of gambling and learning how to manage your emotions, you can avoid tilt and chasing losses, two of the BIGGEST mistakes that can ruin your casino experience.

Chapter 6: Real-World Examples: Success Stories and Lessons Learned

Case Studies: Players Who Beat the Odds

The Blackjack Card-Counting Maestro:

In the bustling heart of Las Vegas, a young mathematician named Alex honed his blackjack skills. Fascinated by the concept of card counting, he meticulously studied books like "Beat the Dealer" by Edward O. Thorp and practiced tirelessly at home. Alex developed a keen eye for recognizing patterns in the dealt cards, allowing him to calculate the probability of the next card being a high or low value.

Armed with this knowledge, Alex ventured into casinos, starting with small bets and gradually increasing them as the count became favorable. He disguised his counting by varying his bets and playing styles, blending in with the crowd. Over time, Alex consistently beat the odds, accumulating a substantial bankroll. His success was not solely due to luck but a result of meticulous study, disciplined execution, and a deep understanding of blackjack probabilities.

The Baccarat Trend Tracker:

Sophia, a shrewd observer with a knack for pattern recognition, found her niche in the elegant world of baccarat. She spent countless hours studying the game, meticulously noting down the results of each hand. Through careful analysis, Sophia discovered subtle trends and patterns in the outcomes, realizing that certain sequences were more likely to occur than others.

Armed with this knowledge, Sophia developed a betting strategy based on trend analysis. She patiently waited for patterns to emerge and placed her bets accordingly. Her disciplined approach and a keen eye for detail paid off handsomely. Over time, Sophia consistently beat the odds, earning a reputation as a baccarat maven.

The Video Poker Strategist:

Michael, a computer programmer with a passion for poker, stumbled upon the world of video poker and was immediately captivated by its blend of skill and chance. He quickly realized that, unlike traditional slot machines, video poker offered the opportunity to make strategic decisions that could influence the outcome of the game.

Michael dove into the world of video poker strategy, analyzing paytables, learning optimal play for different variations, and meticulously calculating expected values. He discovered that some video poker machines, especially those with full-pay tables, offered a positive expected value when played with perfect strategy.

With his newfound knowledge, Michael embarked on a video poker journey, carefully selecting machines with favorable paytables and playing with unwavering discipline. He meticulously tracked his results, adjusting his strategy as needed. His efforts paid off, as he consistently outperformed the house edge and turned video poker into a lucrative hobby.

These real-world examples highlight the diverse paths to success in casino gambling. Whether through card counting in blackjack, trend analysis in baccarat, or strategic play in video poker, these individuals demonstrate that with the right knowledge, skill, and mindset, anyone can improve their chances of beating the odds and walking away a winner.

Common Mistakes: What NOT to Do

While there are many paths to success in the casino, there are also common pitfalls that can quickly derail your efforts. By understanding these mistakes and learning from them, you can avoid falling into the same traps and increase your chances of walking away a winner.

- **Chasing Losses:** One of the most common and destructive mistakes gamblers make is chasing losses. This is a desperate attempt to recoup losses by increasing bets or deviating from a sound strategy. Chasing losses is a slippery slope that can lead to even greater financial ruin. The key is to accept losses as part of the game and never bet more than you can afford to lose.

- **Ignoring Bankroll Management:** Many players fall into the trap of impulsive betting without a clear plan for managing their money. This can lead to overspending, impulsive decisions, and, ultimately, a depleted bankroll. Establishing a strict budget and sticking to it is crucial for long-term success in the casino.
- **Playing Games with High House Edges:** Some casino games are designed to favor the house, with high house edges that make it difficult for players to win in the long run. Avoiding these games and

focusing on those with lower house edges is essential for maximizing your chances of success. Examples of games to avoid include Keno, most slot machines, and American roulette.

- **Gambling While Intoxicated:** Alcohol impairs judgment and decision-making, making it a dangerous companion for gambling. Intoxicated players are more likely to take unnecessary risks, chase losses, and make impulsive bets. It's best to avoid alcohol altogether while gambling or consume it in moderation.
- **Superstitious Beliefs:** Many gamblers fall prey to superstitious beliefs, such as thinking that a machine is "due" for a payout or that a certain ritual will bring them luck. These beliefs are unfounded and can lead to irrational decision-making. Remember, casino games are based on probability and randomness, and there's no way to predict or control the outcome.

Adapting Strategies: Finding What Works for YOU

There's no one-size-fits-all strategy for winning at the casino. What works for one person may not work for another. It's important to experiment with different strategies and find what suits your personality, risk tolerance, and preferred games.

Some players thrive on the excitement of high-stakes games, while others prefer the slow and steady approach of low-stakes games. Some enjoy the social aspect of table games, while others prefer the solitude of video poker machines. There's no right or wrong way to gamble as long as you're doing it responsibly and within your means.

As you gain experience and learn more about different games and strategies, you can start to tailor your approach to fit your individual preferences and goals. Don't be afraid to try new things and step outside your comfort zone. The world of casino gambling is vast and diverse, and there's always something new to discover

Remember, the key to success in the casino is to be adaptable and willing to learn. Continuously refine your strategies, stay informed about the latest trends, and, most importantly, never stop having fun.

Conclusion

There Are No Guarantees: But You Can Tip the Scales

Throughout this book, we've explored a wide range of strategies and insights to help you navigate the thrilling yet often treacherous world of casino gambling. But it's crucial to remember that there are no guarantees in this realm. Lady Luck can be fickle, and even the most skilled players can experience losing streaks.

However, by applying the knowledge and strategies outlined in this book, you can significantly increase your chances of success. You've learned how to choose the right games, manage your bankroll wisely, and make informed betting decisions. You've discovered the importance of discipline, self-control, and a clear understanding of the casino's inherent advantage. By incorporating these principles into your gambling practice, you can tip the scales in your favor and transform a game of chance into a calculated endeavor.

Remember, gambling should be an enjoyable pastime, not a desperate pursuit of riches. Approach the casino with a clear head, a realistic budget, and a willingness to learn and adapt. Don't be afraid to experiment with different strategies and find what works best for you. And most importantly, always gamble responsibly.

Responsible Gambling: The Final Word

As we conclude this journey through the world of casino gambling, it's imperative to reiterate the importance of responsible gambling. Gambling should be a form of entertainment, not a means to an end. Never gamble with money you can't afford to lose, and don't let gambling become a compulsion that consumes your life.

If you feel like you're losing control of your gambling habits, don't hesitate to seek help. There are numerous resources available, including counseling services, support groups, and helplines. Remember, it's never too late to take back control and regain your financial and emotional well-being.

Appendices

Glossary of Casino Terms

- **Bankroll:** The total amount of money a player has set aside for gambling.
- **Bet:** The amount of money wagered on a single hand or spin.
- **Blackjack:** A card game where players try to get a hand value closer to 21 than the dealer without exceeding it.
- **Card Counting:** This strategy is used in blackjack to keep track of the cards that have been dealt and gain an advantage over the house.
- **Comps:** Complimentary goods or services offered by casinos to entice players to gamble more.
- **Expected Value (EV):** The average amount of money a player can expect to win or lose on a particular bet over the long run.
- **House Edge:** The mathematical advantage the casino has over players in a particular game, expressed a a percentage.

- **Payout Percentage:** The percentage of total wagers that a slot machine or other casino game is expected to return to players over time.
- **Random Number Generator (RNG):** A computer program that determines the outcome of each spin on a slot machine or other electronic game.
- **Tilt:** A state of emotional or mental frustration in which a player adopts a less-than-optimal strategy, usually resulting in irrational decision-making and increased losses.

Recommended Reading and Resources

- **Bringing Down the House** by Ben Mezrich: The true story of the MIT Blackjack Team, a group of students who used card counting to win millions of dollars from casinos.
- **The Theory of Poker** by David Sklansky: A comprehensive guide to poker strategy, covering topics like hand selection, betting, and bluffing.
- **Gambling 102: The Best Strategies for All Casino Games** by Michael Shackleford: A detailed analysis of various casino games, including blackjack, baccarat, craps, roulette, and video poker.
- **National Council on Problem Gambling (NCPG):** 1-800-522-4700
- **Gamblers Anonymous International:** www.gamblersanonymous.org
- **Gam-Anon:** www.gam-anon.org
- **National Center for Responsible Gaming (NCRG):** www.ncrg.org

SELF-ASSESSMENT: ARE YOU A RESPONSIBLE GAMBLER

1. Do you gamble more than you can afford to lose?

2. Do you gamble to escape problems or relieve stress?

3. Do you lie to friends and family about your gambling habits?

4. Have you tried to cut back on gambling but been unsuccessful?

5. Have you borrowed money or sold possessions to finance your gambling?

6. Do you feel restless or irritable when you try to stop gambling?

7. Do you gamble until you lose all your money?

8. Have you jeopardized or lost a relationship, job, or educational opportunity because of gambling?

If you answered "yes" to any of these questions, you may have a gambling problem. Seek help from a professional counselor or support group.

Made in United States
Orlando, FL
01 October 2024

52208518R00017